GLEN ROCK PUBLIC LIBRARY
315 ROCK ROAD
GLEN ROCK, N.J. 07452

Discovering Cultures

Ireland

Patricia J. Murphy

BENCHMARK **B**OOKS

MARSHALL CAVENDISH
NEW YORK

For my Irish ancestors, with love—P.J.M.

With thanks to Breandán Mac Suibhne, Program Coordinator, Keough Institute for Irish Studies, University of Notre Dame, for the careful review of this manuscript.

Benchmark Books
Marshall Cavendish
99 White Plains Road
Tarrytown, New York 10591-9001
www.marshallcavendish.com

Text copyright © 2003 by Marshall Cavendish Corporation
Map and illustrations copyright © 2003 by Marshall Cavendish Corporation

All rights reserved. No part of this book may be reproduced or utilized in any form or by any means electronic or mechanical, including photocopying, recording, or by any information storage and retrieval system, without written permission from the copyright holders.

All Internet sites were available and accurate when sent to press.

Library of Congress Cataloging-in-Publication Data

Murphy, Patricia J.
Ireland / by Patricia J. Murphy.
p. cm. — (Discovering cultures)
Summary: Highlights the geography, people, food, schools, recreation, celebrations, and language of Ireland.
Includes bibliographical references and index.
ISBN 0-7614-1515-7
1. Ireland—Juvenile literature. [1. Ireland.] I. Title. II. Series.
DA906 .M87 2004
941.7—dc21   2002015303

Photo Research by Candlepants Incorporated
Cover Photo: Corbis/Charles Philip

The photographs in this book are used by permission and through the courtesy of; *Corbis*: Tim Thompson, 1, 19, back cover; Richard T. Nowitz, 6; Macduff Everton, 8-9; Adam Woolfitt, 10-11, 23, Ric Ergenbright, 12; Michael St. Muir Sheil, 13, 20, 22, 30, 32, 34 (left & right), 45(right); Hugh Rooney:Eye Ubiquitous, 14; Annie Griffiths Belt, 15; Peter Turnley, 16, 40; Jack Fields, 17; Joseph Sohm; ChromoSohm Inc., 18; Richard Cummins, 21; Paul A. Souders, 26, 27; Jim Richardson, 28; David Turnley, 29; Michael Brennen, 33; Patrick Ward, 35; Geray Sweeney, 38-39; Hulton-Deutsch Collection, 44. *Douglas Fountain & Christine Patricia Cullen*, 4-5. *Steven Needham/Envision*, 24. *Photocall Ireland!*, Gareth Chaney, 36; Leon Farrell, 37. *Cameraphoto/Art Resource NY*, 45 (left).

Map and illustrations by Salvatore Murdocca
Book design by Virginia Pope

Cover: *The Irish landscape;* Title page: *An Irish dancer in traditional dress*

Printed in Hong Kong
1 3 5 6 4 2

Turn the Pages...

Where in the World Is Ireland?	6
What Makes Ireland Irish?	14
Living in Ireland	20
School Days	26
Just for Fun	32
Let's Celebrate!	36
The Flag and Money	42
Count in Irish	43
Glossary	43
Proud to Be Irish	44
Find Out More	46
Index	47

Céad míle fáilte (a hundred thousand welcomes) await you in Ireland—along with warm, friendly people, and cool, ocean breezes. And if you like the color green, you are in luck!

Irish eyes smile.

Where in the World Is Ireland?

Ireland is located west of Great Britain. It is surrounded by the Atlantic Ocean on the north, west, and east, and the Irish Sea to the south.

Ireland is divided into two regions: the Republic of Ireland and Northern Ireland. Northern Ireland is a part of the United Kingdom. Its capital is Belfast. The capital of the Republic of Ireland is Dublin. It lies on the River Liffey. One thousand years ago,

Dublin's Custom House is home to Irish government offices.

Dublin was a Viking trading post. Today, it is home to Trinity College, fancy department stores, expensive hotels, fine restaurants, and many museums.

Long ago Ireland and Great Britain were one landmass. During the Ice Age, glaciers shaped the Earth. When the ice melted, the land between Ireland and Great Britain filled with water. Ireland became an island.

Ireland is often compared to a bowl. It is lower in the center and higher around the edges. In the center of the country, there are lowland plains. On these plains there are green meadows, rolling hills, freshwater lakes, forests, bogs, and rich pas-

The Irish countryside

tures. On the higher ground, there are mountain ranges, rugged cliffs, lakes, sand-filled beaches, and harbors. Ireland has 800 lakes. Its largest lake is Lough Neagh. It is 246 square miles (396 square kilometers). The River Shannon is its longest river. It runs 211 miles (340 kilometers). Along Ireland's coasts are many small islands.

Often called the Emerald Isle because of its lush, green landscape, Ireland is a beautiful country. From above, the land looks like a patchwork quilt with forty shades of green. Each patch of green is divided by rows of hedges or stone walls. Sparkling blue lakes, rivers, and streams crisscross the green landscape. Beds of shamrock cover the island.

From north to south, Ireland is 302 miles (486 kilometers) long. From east to west it is 171 miles (275 kilometers) wide. That makes Ireland a *wee* (little) bit bigger than the state of West Virginia, but smaller than Maine. Ireland's highest point is atop Carrantuohill, a mountain in County Kerry. This peak is 3,414 feet (1,041 meters) high.

The climate throughout Ireland is the same from place to place. The southwest wind currents pull warm air up from the Gulf Stream to make it mild. The surrounding Atlantic waters make it damp and often rainy. The Irish often say, "It is either raining — or fixin' to rain." The annual rainfall in Ireland's lowlands is 30 inches (76 centimeters). On high ground,

A green valley by Shannon, Ireland

the annual rainfall is 100 inches (254 centimeters). While it rains most days in Ireland, the days include what the Irish call "sunny spells," or sunshine.

Whether it is rainy or sunny, the weather gives Ireland its magical feel. Without it, Ireland would not have its many shades of green or daily rainbows.

Dunluce Castle in Northern Ireland

The Blarney Stone

Both Irish citizens and tourists enjoy exploring the ruined towers, forts, churches, cemeteries, and magical castles that dot Ireland's landscape. One of the most famous castles is Blarney Castle in southwest Ireland. It is where the legendary Blarney Stone can be found. If someone kisses the Blarney Stone, it is believed he or she will receive the gift of the gab—the ability to speak very well. Kissing this stone, however, is no easy feat. To reach it, kissers must bend over backwards and lower themselves down about two feet from the top of the castle—with help, of course!

What Makes Ireland Irish?

The most important things to the Irish are church, family, and country. More than 90 percent of Irish citizens in the Republic of Ireland are Roman Catholic Christians. The rest are Anglican, Protestant, or Jewish. In Northern Ireland, 58 percent of its citizens are Protestants and 42 percent are Roman Catholic. The Irish are very religious and regularly attend weekly church services. Many of their important holidays begin in church.

The Irish love their families very much. Many young people live with their parents until they marry. Older people who need care live with their relatives, too. If families do

Saint Patrick's Cathedral in Northern Ireland

The O'Sullivan Family

A young girl waves an Irish flag.

not live together, they usually live nearby and get together often.

The Irish love their country, too. Their ancestors fought long and hard for Ireland's freedom. For over 700 years, England ruled over Ireland. The Irish fought for their independence for many years. This fight made the Irish pride very strong.

The Irish are known for their sense of humor and gift of the gab. They love to talk and to tell stories. Some Irish speak both English and Gaelic, Ireland's native language. They inherited Gaelic and the art of storytelling from the Celts, Ireland's first settlers. The Celts told wild stories of fierce battles, brave heroes, and mythical fairies. It was often hard to tell whether their stories were true or make-believe.

Irish stories have inspired popular books, art, and music. Irish writers such as Samuel Beckett and George Bernard Shaw have won Nobel Prizes. Frank McCourt won the Pulitzer Prize.

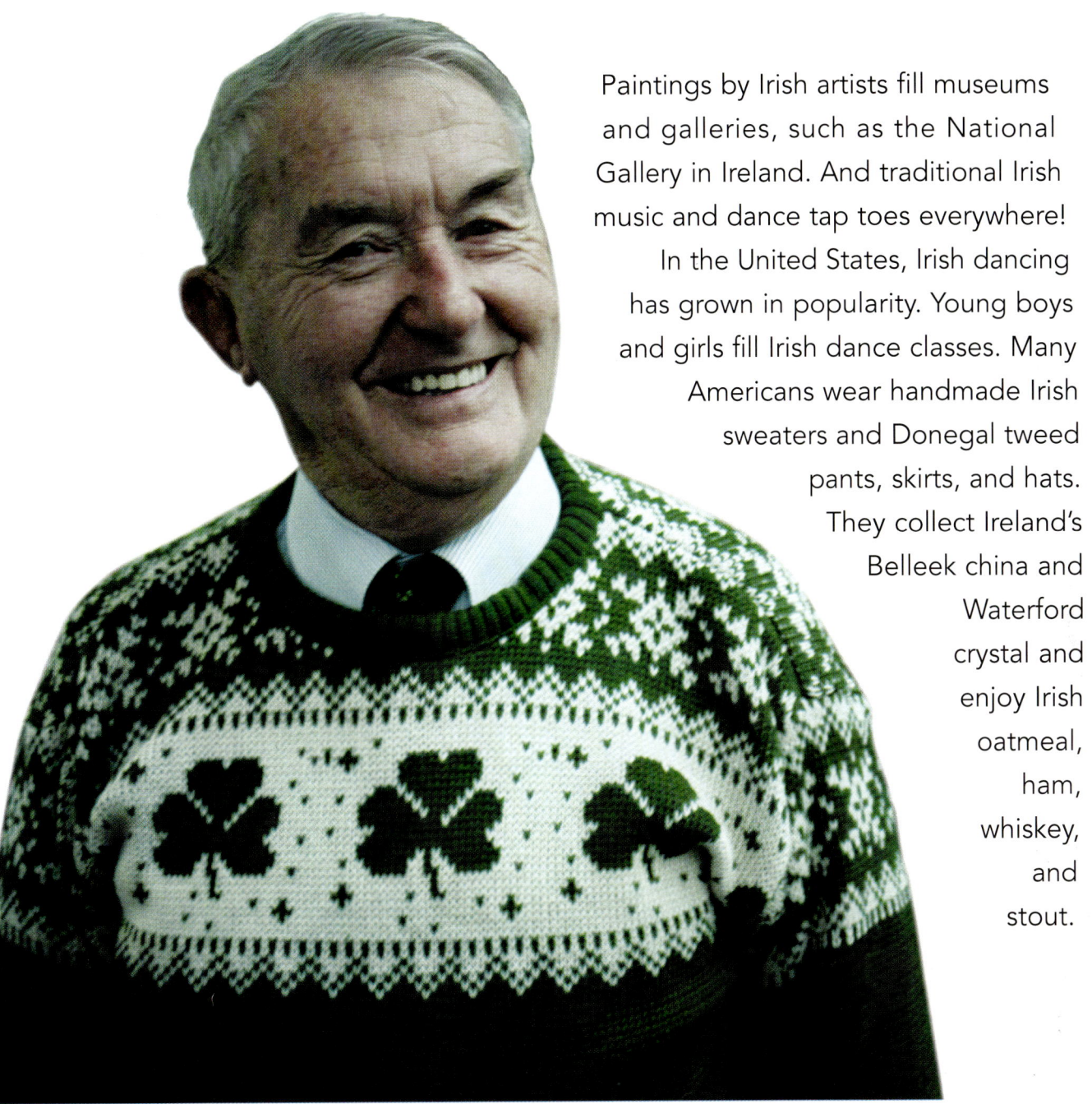

Paintings by Irish artists fill museums and galleries, such as the National Gallery in Ireland. And traditional Irish music and dance tap toes everywhere! In the United States, Irish dancing has grown in popularity. Young boys and girls fill Irish dance classes. Many Americans wear handmade Irish sweaters and Donegal tweed pants, skirts, and hats. They collect Ireland's Belleek china and Waterford crystal and enjoy Irish oatmeal, ham, whiskey, and stout.

The Irish sweater

Bagpipers march in New York's Saint Patrick's Day Parade.

On March 17, many Irish-Americans celebrate Saint Patrick's Day. In fact, there are more people of Irish descent living in the United States than there are in Ireland! They host big Saint Patrick's Day celebrations in New York, Chicago, and Boston. The world's largest is in Savannah, Georgia.

Irish Dancing

Wherever there is Irish music, traditional Irish dancing is not far behind. Irish dancing is all in the feet. To begin, dancers hold their arms and hands close to their sides. They move their feet to the quick beat of the music. Irish dancers wear hard *jig* shoes to perform dances with thunderous steps. They wear soft shoes called *ghillies* or *pumps* to perform dances with small jumps, quick beats, and crossover steps. Their dances are called jigs, reels, hornpipes, and sets. Girls also wear special dresses. These are handmade with lace and Celtic symbols. In the early days, the Irish would dance in front of the fire to the beat of clapping hands or stomping feet. Family members would try to out-step each other. Today, traditional Irish dancing is enjoyed at Irish festivals and dances, and competitions all over the world.

Living in Ireland

Today, there are almost four million people living on the Irish isle. More than 50 percent of them live in or near the cities. The rest live in small towns or villages. City and country life are often very different.

Ireland's capital, Dublin, is a busy city with tall buildings and traffic jams. Many people live in flats, or apartments. Some may own houses outside of the city.

Shoppers crowd Dublin's Grafton Street.

An Irish cottage with a thatched roof

Dubliners may work in Ireland's computer, telecommunications, and tourism industries. Some may work in the brewing industry or in factories that make fine crystal and fabrics. Others join the *garda* (police), or become teachers, nurses, and doctors.

In the country, the Irish live among the rolling green fields, hills, and pastures. Long ago, many people lived in small cottages with thatched roofs. Today, most live in modern farmhouses. Many people burn turf to heat their homes.

Herding cattle

Farmers live in the country. They grow crops or raise sheep and cattle. Ireland's main crops are potatoes, grains, sugar beets, and turnips. The potato has long been an important source of food for the Irish. During the Great Famine of 1845–1851, one million Irish people died when a black fungus destroyed their potato crops. The British government did little to help the starving people. As a result, one million Irish citizens moved to other countries. Today, potatoes are still served with most Irish meals.

In addition to potato and cattle farmers, Ireland has many fishermen. They fish in Ireland's lakes, rivers, and oceans to earn a living. These fishermen catch trout, salmon, cod, mackerel, plaice, and shellfish. Some people in the country and city work in butcher shops, bakeries, and other storefronts. Craftsmen make and sell handmade goods such as famous Irish sweaters or Irish lace.

Wherever people live or work in Ireland, many begin their day with a full Irish breakfast. This meal may include eggs, bacon, sausage, potatoes, tomatoes, black pudding, soda bread, juice, and tea. The next big meal is lunch. People often eat Irish stew with lamb, potatoes, onions, carrots, leeks, and pearl barley. Sandwiches,

An Irish potato farmer tends to his crop.

Irish soda bread, butter, and preserves

cold meats, or fish also may be served for lunch and supper. And every good meal ends with dessert. Scones, tarts, and cakes are among Irish favorites. Later in the evening, many Irish head to local pubs. There, they visit with friends, listen to music, and relax with cool drinks.

Let's Eat!
Irish Soda Bread

The Irish love to eat soda bread with their meals. It is best when made with buttermilk, and enjoyed with a cup of Irish tea. Ask an adult to help you prepare this recipe.

Ingredients:

4 cups sifted all-purpose flour

1/4 cup granulated sugar

1 teaspoon salt

1 teaspoon baking powder

1 teaspoon baking soda

2 tablespoons caraway seeds

1 1/3 cups buttermilk

1/4 cup butter

1 egg (unbeaten)

1 egg yoke (beaten)

1/2 cup raisins or currants, if desired

Wash your hands. In a bowl, sift together the flour, sugar, salt, and baking powder. Stir in caraway seeds. Cut butter into small pieces and add to mixture. Combine buttermilk, egg, and baking soda, and stir into flour mixture. Add raisins or currants. Place dough on a floured board. Knead until dough is smooth. Form dough into one round loaf—about two inches high. Use a knife to make a large "X" on the top of your dough. Brush with egg yolk. Bake on a greased cooking sheet at 375 degrees Fahrenheit (191 degrees Celsius) for 70 minutes or until done. Allow to cool. Serve with butter and preserves. Makes one loaf.

School Days

The Irish value education. They believe that it makes their country strong and their future bright. In Ireland, school is free. All children in the Republic of Ireland must attend school from the ages of six to fifteen. Most of them, however, begin

An Irish lad giggles in school.

A smiling schoolgirl

school as early as four or five years old and continue through college. In Northern Ireland, children must go to school from the ages of four to sixteen. The Irish school day is usually six to seven hours long, Monday through Friday. School breaks are held in the summer, fall, and winter.

Irish students in matching uniforms

At most Irish schools, children wear uniforms. Sometimes, these uniforms are pullover sweaters or vests worn with skirts or pants. Other times, they may include dark jackets and ties. All children learn to speak and write English and Irish. They also study literature, writing, math, music, art, history, the environment, foreign languages, and computers. Most Irish schools are also connected to the Internet.

Inside an Irish classroom

Primary school lasts eight years. After finishing primary school, most Irish children attend a secondary school. This school has two parts called "cycles." The junior cycle takes three years to complete. It is like junior high in the United States. Junior cycle studies include language, science, art, music, Irish, English, math, history, and geography. After the junior cycle, students must take an exam called the Junior Certificate.

An Irish dancer performs a jig.

The senior cycle is like high school in the United States. During the two-year senior cycle, students prepare for their Leaving Certificate exam. This exam tests students on what they have learned. Upon passing the Leaving Certificate, many Irish students attend a university, technical college, or college of education.

After school hours, some children take Irish dancing or horseback-riding lessons. Many also help with chores around the house or with the family farm or store. Others enjoy singing, shopping, playing sports, and hanging out with friends.

Irish Eyes

This Irish song is a favorite among the old and young in Ireland.

Just for Fun

Playing or listening to music are favorite Irish pastimes. Irish music almost always leads to dancing—another favorite. The Irish have enjoyed music and dance for centuries. In fact, they love music so much that the harp is a national symbol. Today musicians use traditional musical instruments such as the *bodhrán* (a hand drum) and modern instruments such as the guitar to create popular Irish music. When the Irish get tired of music and dance, there is always a story about a leprechaun or a legendary hero to retell!

The harp is a national symbol in Ireland.

Horseback riding along the Irish coast

Outdoors, Ireland's countryside offers people miles and miles to walk, hike, bike, fish, sail, golf, and ride horseback. Ireland's scenic coasts, quaint villages, and lively cities are hot spots for holiday travel. The Irish also travel to Spain and other European countries for vacation.

Irish people enjoy watching and playing sports such as Gaelic football, hurling, *camogie* (women's hurling), rugby, and soccer. Gaelic football and hurling are the most popular sports in Ireland. Gaelic football is similar to soccer, except players can handle the ball. Hurling is a lot like field hockey, but much faster. Gaelic football and hurling teams from different parishes and counties compete in all-Irish championships. Ireland's soccer teams have competed in European and

Irish fans cheer on their hurling team.

Rugby players battle it out.

world championships. Irish golfers, cyclists, boxers, runners, and jockeys have won many championships and earned the country several Olympic medals.

Ireland's greyhound and horse racing draw big crowds. The Irish are known for their world-class racehorses and for the Irish Derby horse race held each spring. In Ireland, there are 240 days of racing!

Leprechauns

The Irish love their stories and legends. They enjoy telling a tale or two especially if those tales include leprechauns. Leprechauns are legendary Irish fairies. These fairies are known to guard the pots of gold at the end of rainbows. While they are little and cute, they are not entirely nice. They do not want you or anyone else to get their pots of gold. If you do happen to catch a leprechaun, he is sure to trick you to look away. If you do, he will vanish with a blink of an eye along with your chance for the gold.

Fairy forts can be found throughout Ireland. These are places in the countryside where the Irish believe leprechauns live. Some bushes, or structures made of stone or earth, are thought to be fairy forts. Great care is taken not to disturb them while repairing a road or building a house. For if you tear a fairy fort down, who knows what a leprechaun might do!

Let's Celebrate!

Most of Ireland's holidays and festivals involve family and religion. Their biggest holidays include Christmas, Easter, and Saint Patrick's Day. Each of these holidays begins with church services, and ends with big meals and time spent with family and friends.

Singers at a Christmas church service

Each Christmas, the Irish put candles in their windows. These candles are said to light the way for Mary, Joseph, and baby Jesus on Christmas Eve. They also clean their homes. Some even whitewash or paint the outside of their houses. The Irish also trim their trees with lights, tinsel, and ornaments. They display wreaths, ivy, garland, and nativity cribs in their homes. And Irish children hang stockings above the fireplace.

Many Irish attend Midnight Mass on Christmas Eve. When Christmas Day arrives, they exchange gifts and enjoy turkey, ham, spiced beef, stuffing, cranberry sauce, mince pies, and plum pudding.

A visit with Santa

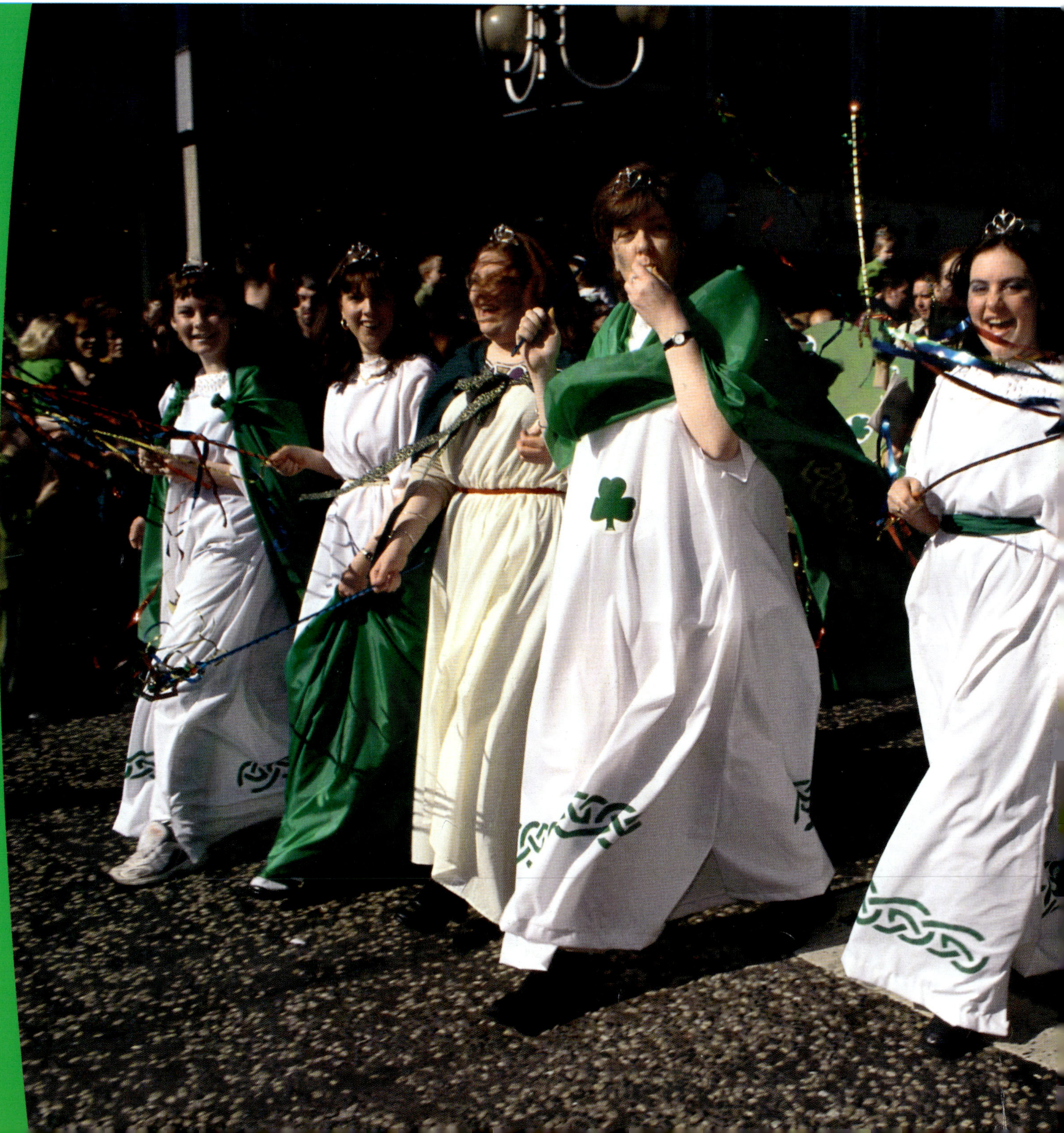

The celebrating continues until the sixth of January.

Easter is a more solemn holiday than Christmas. After forty days of Lent, the Irish celebrate the rebirth of Christ. On Easter Sunday, the Irish attend church services and share a hearty family meal. Children decorate and eat eggs.

Saint Patrick's Day is a national holiday in Ireland. It is celebrated on March 17 in honor of Ireland's patron saint, Saint Patrick. It marks the day of Saint Patrick's death. After church services on Saint Patrick's Day, the Irish play music and dance. They march in parades and celebrate in

Saint Patrick's Day parade in Belfast

"Happy Saint Paddy's Day!"

the streets. Dublin City has the biggest parade with marching and brass bands, floats, Irish dancers, and majorettes. On this day, people may say things like "Erin Go Braugh" (Ireland forever) and "Happy Saint Paddy's Day!"

Saint Stephen's Day

The day after Christmas, the Irish celebrate Saint Stephen's Day, also called Wren's Day. It is said that on Saint Stephen's Day a wren betrayed an Irish army by pecking crumbs on a drum in an enemy camp and waking the sleeping soldiers. Another story claims that a wren betrayed Saint Stephen when he was in hiding. And in Irish folklore, the wren is said to have beaten the eagle in a contest to become the king of the birds.

To mark Saint Stephen's Day, Catholic boys dress as wren boys. Wren boys wear unusual clothes, including traditional straw suits and hats. They often wear masks or paint their faces. They go door-to-door saying, "The wren, the wren, the king of the birds." They also sing songs to raise money for charity. At most homes, the boys are served drinks or pudding. Young people at each home are encouraged to join in the fun!

The Irish flag has three vertical stripes—green, white, and orange. The green represents the Irish Catholic roots of Ireland. The orange represents the Protestant roots. The white represents the promise of peace between the two.

Ireland is a member of the European Union (EU). In January 2002, Ireland and eleven other states within the EU began to use the same currency, or money. This currency is called the euro. Euro coins share common European designs on the front, but the designs on the back of the coins change from nation to nation. Euro banknotes, or paper money, are the same in all twelve nations.

Count in Irish

English	Irish	Say it like this:
one	a haon	A HANE
two	a dó	A DOUGH
three	a trí	A TCHREE
four	a ceathair	A CA-her
five	a cúig	A KOO-ig
six	a sé	A SHAY
seven	a seacht	A SHOCKT
eight	a hocht	A HUCTH
nine	a naoi	A KNEE
ten	a deich	A JYE

Glossary

black pudding Type of sausage served with breakfast.
bog Area of wet, spongy land where people dig turf.
céad míle fáilte (KADE MEE-la FWAL-teh) One hundred thousand welcomes.
patron saint Saint who looks over a particular country or group of people.
plaice Type of fish found in Irish waters. Called flounder in the United States.
shamrock Small green plant with three leaves; a national symbol of Ireland.
stout Dark ale or alcohol with a malty taste.
thatched Covered with grass.
turf Plant matter cut from bogs, dried, and burned as fuel; also called peat.
tweed Rough wool cloth woven with yarns of two or more colors.

Proud to Be Irish

James Joyce (1882–1941)

James Joyce was born in 1882 in Dublin, Ireland. Before Joyce became one of the greatest novelists of the twentieth century, he wrote book reviews, taught school, and worked in a bank. Joyce wrote about the people of Dublin in a series of short stories called *Dubliners*. In his most famous novel, *Ulysses*, readers follow the character, Leopold Bloom, through the day, June 16, 1904, in Dublin. Today, people celebrate "Bloomsday" on June 16 to honor Joyce and Bloomsday.

Mary Robinson (1944–)

Mary Robinson was born in Ballina, County Mayo, Ireland in 1944. She became Ireland's first woman president on December 3, 1990. Before she became president, she was a lawyer and a law professor at Trinity

College in Dublin. While president, Ms. Robinson worked hard to help solve social problems in her country. In 1997, she left office to work for the United Nations as the High Commissioner for Human Rights.

Saint Patrick (approximately 389—461)

According to Irish legend, Saint Patrick brought Christianity to Ireland. He was born in Britain and kidnapped by Irish raiders at the age of sixteen. He spent six years in captivity in Ireland. When he escaped, he had visions telling him to return to Ireland to teach people about Christianity. It is said that Saint Patrick used a shamrock plant to explain the Christian belief in the Holy Trinity—the Father, the Son, and the Holy Spirit. This is how the shamrock became an important symbol in Ireland.

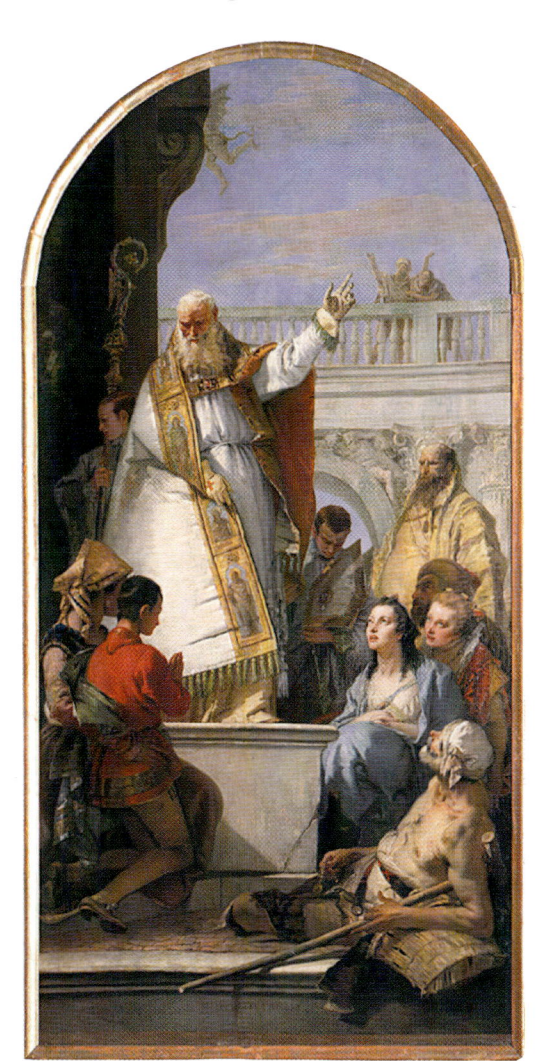

Find Out More

Books

Ireland: Faces and Places by Patrick Ryan. The Child's World, Minnesota, 2000.

Ireland by Patrick Daley. Raintree Steck-Vaughn, New York, 2002.

Look What Came from Ireland by Miles Harvey. Franklin Watts, New York, 2001.

Ireland by Joanne Mattern. Bridgestone Books, Minnesota, 2003.

Web sites

Search **www.irelandseye.com** to learn more about Irish culture, history and traditions.

Go to **http://www.irelandemb.org/links.html** for the Irish Embassy in Washington, D.C.

For more information about Ireland and links to other on-line sources visit **http://www.yahooligans.com/around_the_world/countries/Ireland/**.

Video

Patrick: Brave Shepherd of the Emerald Isle. Creative Communications Center, N.V., Irving, TX: CCM of America, 1993.

Index

Page numbers for illustrations are in **boldface.**

maps
    Ireland, 7

architecture, **4–5**, **6**, **12**, **14**
art, 17

beaches, 9
Belfast, 6, **38–39**
Blarney stone, 13, **13**

castles, **12**, 13
cathedrals, **14**
cities, 6, 20.
    See also Belfast; Dublin
clothing/costumes, 17, **17**, 19, **19**, 28, **28**, **30**, **38–39**, 41, 43

dance, 17, 19, **19**, 30, **30**, 39–40
Dublin, **6**, 6–8, **20**, 20–21, 40, 44

education, 8, 26–30. **26**, **27**, **28**, **29**
England, 6, 22
European Union, 42

family, 14–16, **15**, 19
famine, 22
farming, 22, **22**, **23**
fishing, 22, 43
flag, **42**
food, 17, 22, 23–25, **24**, 37–39, 41, 43

government, 6, **6**
greetings, 4, 40, 43

history, 6–8, 16, 22
holidays, 14, 18, **18**, **36**, 36–41, **37**, **38–39**, **40**
horses, **33**, 34
houses, **4–5**, 20, 21, **21**, 37, 43
humor, 16

Ice Age, 8

jobs, 21, 22
Joyce, James, 44, **44**

lakes, 8, 9
land, **8–9**, 8–10, **10–11**, 20–22, **21**, 35, 43
language, 16, 28, 43
legends, 13, **13**, 16, 35, 41, 45
leprechauns, 35
location, 6

marshland (bogs), 8, 43
money, 42, **42**
mountains, 9, 10
museums, 6–8, 17
music, 17, **18**, 31–32, **32**, 39–40

name, 9
Northern Ireland, 6, **12**, 14

patriotism, 16, **16**, 39–40, 43
people, **4–5**, 13, 14–16, **15**, **26**, **27**, 30
plants (shamrock), 10, 43, 45
population, 18, 20
presidents, 44–45
products, 17, **17**, 22, **23**

recipe, **24**, 25
regions, 6
religion, 14, **14**, 42, 43.
    See also holidays
Republic of Ireland, 6
rivers, 6, 9
Robinson, Mary, 44–45, **45**

Saint Patrick, 45, **45**.
    See also holidays
Saint Stephen, 41
shopping, 6–8, **20**
size, 10
songs/singing, 31, **36**, 41
sports, 33–34, **34**
storytelling, 16, 32
symbols, 43, 45

vacations, 33

weather, 10–12
Web sites, 46
women, 44–45
writers, 16, 44

47

About the Author

Patricia J. Murphy writes children's storybooks, nonfiction books, early readers, and poetry. She also writes for magazines, corporations, educational publishing companies, and museums.

Patricia lives in Northbrook, IL, USA. Her ancestors are from the Counties of Mayo and Roscommon in the Republic of Ireland. She travels to the Emerald Isle every October with her family. Each time she returns to Ireland, she feels like she has come home.

Acknowledgments

Special thanks to John O'Grady, Gaelic teacher at the Irish Heritage Center, Chicago, IL; The Trinity Irish Dance Company; the Irish Embassy and the Irish Tourism Council; and my parents who have shared Ireland with me.